The
Inward Journey

Discovering
Your Spiritual Self

Marilyn Norquist Gustin

D0377072

LIGUORI
PUBLICATIONS

One Liguori Drive
Liguori, Missouri 63057-9999
(314) 464-2500

Imprimi Potest:
James Shea, C.SS.R.
Provincial, St. Louis Province
The Redemptorists

Imprimatur:
Monsignor Maurice F. Byrne
Vice Chancellor, Archdiocese of St. Louis

ISBN 0-89243-334-5
Library of Congress Catalog Card Number: 90-63731

Scripture selections are taken from the NEW AMERICAN BIBLE WITH
REVISED NEW TESTAMENT, copyright © 1986, by the Confraternity
of Christian Doctrine, Washington, DC, and are used by permission
of copyright owner. All rights reserved.

Cover and interior design by Pam Hummelsheim

CONTENTS

FOREWORD

A foreword lets the reader in on the style and themes of the pages that follow. As editor-in-chief of the *Liguorian,* I am privileged to write the foreword to *The Inward Journey.*

This book began as a series in the *Liguorian* magazine. The response to Marilyn Norquist Gustin's articles was overwhelmingly positive. Our readers found the series to be an excellent instruction and recommended it to those seeking a deeper walk with the Lord.

Human life has a beginning and an end. That interval between birth and death is a journey back to God. On that journey we have a spiritual heritage that we want not only to honor but also to understand more deeply. We want our religious truths to guide us on that journey. Those spiritual awakenings reach all corners of ourselves. They give us insight, raise questions, and make us see ourselves in new ways. What good qualities lie within us? How do we choose to use them today? These simple questions point the way and give us the opportunity to change our lives, to be the kind of person we want to be at this moment, and to learn from today's experiment in living.

We look upon Marilyn's articles as touchstones in that spiritual journey. We all have touchstones in our lives — our principles, a word from a friend, a favorite quotation that guides our lives and against which we measure thoughts and actions. They provide a solid base for living and are a tangible reminder of the truth. The articles on spirituality served as touchstones for *Liguorian* readers. They brought us out of our confusion and served as an external reference point helping us recall the path and return to it. Our hope is that this book will serve that same purpose for you.

Allan Weinert, C.SS.R.

CHAPTER ONE

Spirituality:
Our Inward Journey

pirituality is fast becoming a word that is more confusing than helpful. Under its umbrella we find psychology, social action, marriage and child-rearing, and other segments of life. It is true that all these — every moment of living, in fact — are ideally included in the spiritual life. But if we try to think about them all at once, we only become less clear about spirituality itself.

The Inward Journey

This book is about Christian spiritual life. Saint Bonaventure, the great Franciscan of the thirteenth century, defined spiritual life as "the inward journey of the soul into God."

Three points stand out in this brief definition. First, the essence of spirituality is inward; it is within us. It is the transformation that happens in our hearts and minds, our deepest being, so we gradually enter the heart of God himself.

We are, however, beings with physical bodies. The physical world cannot be ignored in spirituality, even though the essence of the spirit is interior. All our outward behavior, our relationships and activities, participate in our spirituality. Inner changes spill over into the outer world as natural expressions of our spiritual growth. For example, if we discover a new peace in our hearts, we will act more peacefully toward others. Further, outward things can either support the interior journey or not support it. Those behaviors that support the interior life are part of our spirituality.

The second main point in Bonaventure's definition is that the spiritual life is a journey. We do not get to the goal all at once. We travel along step by step as each new change is shown to us and we can accept each new gift. We may take side trips too, although the great inward travelers suggest we avoid them.

Mainly, we must recognize that spiritual life is a process. That process is not the same for everyone, except in broad outline.

Certain changes do happen for each pilgrim, but the form in which they come and the way they are expressed differ in each life. It is important that we accept our own experience of the path, the one that is valid for us. After all, God is guiding our spiritual growth and he knows what is most helpful for us.

Oneness With God

The third main point in Bonaventure's definition is that this journey goes "into God." The journey into God is the process by which we become truly like Christ so, as we pray in every celebration of the Eucharist, we can "participate in the divinity of Christ."

For the first several centuries of the Church, Christians understood that Christ became human so "humans can become God." Saints Athanasius, Irenaeus, Gregory of Nyssa, and others said it exactly that way. By God's grace we can become so transformed that we are like Jesus Christ. We can become incorporated into him so that we are one with him and one with God.

We find this certainty in the Gospel of John. Jesus says, "As you, Father, are in me and I in you, that they also may be in us…I in them and you in me" (17:21, 23). The unity of disciple, Christ, and the Father is a powerful theme in John. It is not a figure of speech; it is the goal of every Christian spiritual life. If it seems bold, perhaps that is only because we have for so long ignored it and put off transformation until after death.

The spiritual process leading to oneness with God has certain characteristics. First, spiritual growth is actual experience. It is not mainly words or theories. It is experience we can feel and know, even more powerfully than one can describe it.

When we enter the spiritual journey, we can expect to experience life differently. We can expect to be changed, inwardly first and then on the outside. Our beliefs will support us, but they are not the main element. The main ingredient is what Christ in God gives us to experience and grow from our own lives.

A Magnificent Adventure

Those of us who sincerely participate in this process find that spiritual growth is the most magnificent adventure imaginable. It is full of fascinating events and challenging possibilities.

Several years ago I received a set of tapes on the spiritual life. The first thirty minutes of the talks were filled with words like *suffering, difficult, painful, hard, struggle.* But, the speaker said, we must do it because it is the right thing, because Christ said so. Before long I was feeling "Who wants it?" The notion that spirituality is filled with suffering is wrong.

The spiritual life is, in fact, an astounding quest. Every day will show its newness and freshness. Healing and comfort, blazing insight and strength, all come in their proper places. The human heart discovers its own splendid peacefulness. That peace is dynamic and flowing, like a fountain of living water springing up in the heart. (See John 4:14.)

The spiritual life is grounded in joy — God's very heart overflowing into our own. Jesus taught that his joy would be our joy and our joy would be complete. The more we open up to God's joy, the more we receive it — until our life is always joyful.

Moreover, we discover love. When we are still, even if circumstances are unpleasant, we can locate within us that silent point where love always lives. Increasingly, we discover the actuality of the claim that the Holy Spirit lives in us.

Our interior journey into God is lit by peace, joy, and love. Life brings difficulties and pain. The spiritual process does not waste them but uses them for God's own joyful purposes in our hearts. Obstacles become steppingstones, bringing us closer to God. We begin to welcome them as we learn that on the other side of the obstacles our joy deepens, our peace broadens out like a lake, and we experience more vitally the love of God.

The Image of God

We are made in the image of God. (See Genesis 1:27.) That means that at the very center of our being something of God lives like a tiny flame. It seems tiny because it is hidden from us by layers of selfishness. In reality that image within us contains all that God is. The spiritual journey is a process of uncovering that incredible greatness of God in our hearts. He waits for us to find him there.

In this sense everything that happens in the spiritual life aims at removing one more layer of grime — some mystics have called it outright filth — until nothing stands between our awareness and that fullness of life and love that is God himself. Thus understood, spirituality is an undoing more than it is a doing.

The undoing centers around one issue: our selfishness, our ego-centeredness, the part of us that cries, "Me! Mine! Keep!" This portion of ourselves must gradually be unwound from its grip on our heart so our heart can open fully to the God within us.

The ego-mind is usually in total control of our lives. We tend to believe it is all there is to us. That is an error. The spiritual life is the process by which we put the ego-mind in its proper place. It is a tool for life in the world, but it must be removed from its domineering position.

Together with God we gradually oust the ego from its number one spot and put it quietly beside us, to be called upon when needed. Step by step God enters the number one spot, and we become free in him, full of him, one with him.

This possibility is the Christian invitation. It is the reason for Christ's coming. It is the purpose of God's creation of us. We may have forgotten it, but we can remember and begin the joyful trek homeward. We are invited to "the inward journey of the soul into God" so we may be one with him, now and forever.

For Your Reflection

1. What have I assumed about spiritual life? What is it? Is union with God possible for me?
2. Am I genuinely interested in spirituality or only in certain religious habits?
3. Would I want closeness to God if I could have it? Is it just another "should"? Am I afraid of it?
4. Here are Scripture references that could prove helpful.

   Romans 12:2
   2 Peter 1:3-4
   Psalm 112:1
   Isaiah 55:10-13
   John 14:20; 17:21-26
   Luke 1:46-47
   Psalms 70:5-7; 72:5
   1 John 2:5-6; 3:14; 4:7-13, 16-19

CHAPTER TWO

Grace and Personal Effort: Partners on the Journey

It was a puzzle. I was reading the lives and writings of the Christian mystics, the saints who experienced union with God. They all said, "It is all grace. Everything in spiritual life is grace." This seemed to mean that God gave freely to those he chose.

Yet in the lives of these great mystics, it was obvious they all worked diligently at their spiritual life. They practiced mortification, they prayed for hours, they sacrificed, and they served constantly. It certainly appeared they earned what they eventually experienced in God. Yet they said their effort was nothing.

This seemed to imply that no matter how hard a person works at it, life with God is only given to the mysteriously chosen. That sounded rather hopeless, at least for me, because I surely had no sense of being specially chosen.

Understanding was years in coming. Now I would like to share what I have learned and experienced about personal effort and the grace of God as they interact in our spiritual growth. The truth, illogical as it may seem, is that they are partners. Both are necessary, but they are not equal.

All Is Grace

The saints are right — grace is everything. Without the sustaining grace of God in our lives at every moment, we would go poof, right out of existence. Without God's gracious breath we would never have known life. In fact, we breathe in grace and walk in grace and make love in grace and sleep in grace. God's grace — his own blessed, completely unearned love and sustenance and help — streams constantly through every being in the universe. God acts graciously because it is his nature to do so. The nonstop flow of his grace into our world and our lives does not depend on us. We can neither stop it nor begin it.

In the personal realm, however, God's grace cannot be fully effective without our cooperation. This is because God gave us a free will in the very act of creation. So for us God's grace accomplishes the most when we welcome it, receive it freely, cooperate with it, and allow it to fulfill itself within us.

If I worked hard all my life, did all the "right" things, I could not bootstrap my way into union with God or participation in Christ's own divine life. Union with God requires God's giving of himself.

The reverse is also true. He can give himself without pause forever, and we will be no closer to him unless we actively cooperate with his grace. God never forces us. He leaves us free to say our yes or no. But the goal of union takes two.

The Spirit at Work

When we feel a desire to journey inward into God, we are already touched by grace. The desire for God is itself a gift of God.

If we make our own effort to cooperate, the transforming process will begin. Receiving grace for the spiritual life is different from our receiving grace in order to breathe. Breathing is automatic. For the spiritual journey, we must receive consciously.

Saint Gregory of Nyssa describes beautifully how divine grace and human response together bring fullness of union with God. He says that in the moment we recognize God's gracious invitation within us, we have the greatest free choice we can ever make. We are free to accept or reject God's initiative. If we say yes, we create a little space in our hearts where the Spirit can begin to work as never before, and our interior journey will begin.

God responds to our yes by filling that little space with himself while at the same time enlarging it. We experience this presence of God as a deep peace and an increased longing for more of God within our hearts. That longing is like a larger space. God responds by filling this space too and again enlarging it. We experience more peace (or joy or contentment or love) and more longing for God.

So it goes, like a spiral coiling into the very heart of God. Notice that, according to Saint Gregory, the active work is done by the grace within us. Our conscious cooperation is to recognize it, receive it openly, rejoice in it, and say yet another longing yes. God's grace does the rest.

This pattern will remain to the highest reaches of our interior transformation into God, into infinity, because God is infinite.

Open to His Grace

Thus we are all receivers. Receptivity does not mean passivity. It takes energy to remain open to receive anything in life. To be open in human relationships or to new experiences requires effort. To receive the wonders of creation takes attention and alertness — effort. We never receive inertly, like vegetables. So, likewise, we must be active in our spiritual efforts.

A true yes to spiritual life is more complex than opening our mouths to say the word. God gives us the impulse, we contribute our efforts, and God brings them to fruition. All three steps are necessary. The middle one is our yes.

The fascinating testimony of the great mystical saints is that no matter how hard they worked, the fruits they experienced were always greater than anything they had ever dreamed. Their efforts seemed nothing at all in comparison with what they received. That is why they could so easily say, "Everything is grace."

Even our effort is supported by grace, but we usually do not recognize this until the journey gets difficult. In the beginning stages, it is enough to know that God supports us in every way we can possibly receive. He guides us and aids us. No one wants us to become one with Christ more than the Father does. It is never God who holds back. If there is any holding back, it is always our own.

Step Into the Circle

Since we know we must do something in order to receive God's grace for this journey, how can we begin?

Beginning the spiritual journey is rather like stepping into a circle. Wherever we step in, if we keep walking, eventually all of the circle is traveled. For an easy step in, we can begin by cultivating three particular attitudes in our heart: gratitude, acceptance, and expectancy.

Gratitude

Grace flows constantly. To let it flow fully through our own being, something must flow outward again. That something is gratitude, and it is completely accessible to every human being. Grace flows into our hearts and lives; gratitude flows back to God.

We all know that our lives are full of things to be grateful for. Some feel grateful quite naturally and easily. Others take life for granted and rarely give thanks. But we can all deepen our gratitude.

We can practice it. We can make a conscious effort, take some time, pay attention *on purpose* to the gratitude in our hearts. We can express it more often. We can open ourselves to feeling it more deeply. We can count our blessings — old but useful advice.

Gratitude connects us to the source of all goodness in our living, and that source is also our goal in the spiritual journey. Ephesians 5:18-20 says, "…be filled with the Spirit, addressing one another [in] psalms and hymns and spiritual songs, singing and playing to the Lord in your hearts, giving thanks always and for everything in the name of our Lord Jesus Christ to God the Father." This is the best way to keep God's grace flowing into our lives.

Acceptance

Our second attitude is acceptance. Once we have given a serious yes to the transforming work of God within, our lives will not be the same. From that moment the Spirit gives only and exactly what is needed for our newborn spiritual life to grow.

This means no matter how strange or wonderful or uncomfortable circumstances may be, they always bear a gift for our journey. It is our task to accept each circumstance and seek the gift. We can be sure the gift will be there. We may have to seek deeply, but in God's gracious economy for the journey to him, nothing — not one single thing — is wasted.

In situations of great happiness, his gift may be reassurance and comfort. In troubles, the gift may be growth in strength. Knowing this, we practice accepting cheerfully and gratefully everything he gives. It may not always be easy, but it will always be worth it.

One of the often unanticipated delights is the discovery of how constant is God's care for our spiritual well-being. Every day, every hour, there are gifts. In time acceptance will become a permanent stance in our hearts, so that we steadily accept all that comes to us.

Expectancy

As we experience this more and more, the third attitude arises in us — expectancy. If we have been alert to God's gifts for a few weeks, for example, we begin to wake up in the morning wondering what today will bring. We can cultivate this feeling by asking God, "What gift do you have for me today?" and eagerly looking for it. We become like children on Christmas morning, sparkling with anticipation of the goodness about to be revealed to us.

With such an expectant attitude — even before our morning coffee — life becomes the stunning and grace-filled adventure with God that it was meant to be from the first day of creation.

For Your Reflection

1. Do I resist God by thinking I must do it all myself?
2. In what ways do I already consciously depend on grace?
3. Do I experience a lot of gratitude? If not, what is blocking it in me?
4. In which circumstances have I found God's gift? In which have I not looked for it?
5. Here are Scripture references that might prove helpful for thought.

   Isaiah 55:1-3a
   John 15:15-16
   Galatians 6:6-9
   Ephesians 4:1-3; 2:4-10; 5:18b-20
   Psalms 42:9; 84:12
   Job 2:10
   Wisdom 3:9
   2 Corinthians 4:15-18; 12:7b-10
   2 John 1:3
   Revelation 22:21
   Daniel 3:89-90
   Sirach 32:14

CHAPTER THREE

The Choice

How do we know when we are ready to begin our interior journey with God? Since many of us still feel there must be a great sign or that we must first be more perfect, we shun the inner journey as desirable but not for us — yet.

It's true that for some, God may do unmistakable "skywriting." But we need not exclude ourselves from seeking spiritual depths just because we don't see a sign in our own sky. It is also true that certain growth must begin before deeper things can take place. If we say yes to God's invitation now, our growth will happen at exactly the right time for us. God will see to that.

God's Gentle Nudge

Most of the time God's invitation to a deeper experience of him comes in very simple ways. Questions may nag us: What am I doing with my life? Who am I anyway? Or a spark might leap in us when we hear about a great saint. Some may experience a deep recurring ache like a hunger or a thirst. God calls still others by awakening a vigorous interest in prayer.

Whatever form God's invitation takes, if it persists we can be sure he is inviting us to enter our personal journey into his heart. This is an invitation, not a command. God will not force us to accept.

Our response to God's invitation should never be a casual one. Whether we say yes or no, we should give our reply genuine, conscious consideration. A half-baked response is not acceptable. "I wish you were either cold or hot....Because you are lukewarm... I will spit you out of my mouth" (Revelation 3:15-16). In modern language we either "go for it" with God or we decline.

Calculating the Cost

Jesus asks, "Which of you wishing to construct a tower does not first sit down and calculate the cost to see if there is enough for its completion?" (Luke 14:28). Before we begin our spiritual journey, we, too, need to ponder our investment. We begin by asking ourselves four important questions.

- What goal do we seek?
- Are we willing to invest actual time and effort in the process?
- What will a deeper spiritual life cost us?
- What benefits and supports can we expect along the way?

Our goal, of course, is to become so deeply one with Christ that he and the Father will "make [their] dwelling" with us (John 14:23). What does full and permanent union with the Father in Christ mean in our daily living experience?

The saints assure us of wonderful qualities of life: peace that stays constant in all circumstances; joy that bubbles up in us, pervading our whole being and steadying us; love that melts the heart and flows generously and unrestricted into the world for its benefit; the disappearance of negative emotions like fear and anger and inferiority feelings; and a vast tenderness that gazes at the world without worry. These are all rewards of oneness with God. They are a part of the goal itself.

Do we want such a life — and are we willing to invest time and energy in seeking it? The spiritual life will not proceed without these investments. We will not be dragged, even willingly, into God's life.

Finding Time

First, we must set aside a special time of solitude and quiet to be with God in prayer. If we wanted to learn French, we would have to devote at least an hour a day to the project. Likewise, if we want to journey to God, we need that daily time.

Our mind immediately objects, "But I don't have time for another project!" If that is actually true, then you may not desire to say yes to the invitation right now. More likely it is not an accurate assessment. Since I have no children, I used to hesitate to tell parents they could find time if they genuinely wanted to. I hesitated, that is, until I heard about Susanna Wesley. She had seventeen children, yet she spent at least one hour a day in quiet prayer. She'd sit in her kitchen chair, throw her apron over her head, and woe to the child who disturbed her!

Television is a voracious consumer of our time. If we can spend an hour a day watching TV, we can find an hour a day for prayer. Or we can sacrifice a little sleep and pray in the early morning. If we get up an hour before the household awakens, and if we do this daily, God will meet us then. He does not sleep.

Jesus tells us, "Seek first the kingdom [of God]…and all these things will be given you besides" (Matthew 6:33). Seeking "all these things" takes effort. It means consciously choosing love over anger or peace over disturbance. Nothing in the spiritual life is automatic. All must be chosen and all must be included in our striving.

Giving Up Selfishness

The most encompassing description of the cost of the spiritual journey is one word — *selfishness*. Every variety of laziness, egocentricity, pride, and selfishness will sooner or later have to be sacrificed. God will give himself totally only to the one who is totally given over to him.

At the beginning this is unimaginable. We know some of our selfish qualities, but we are blind to most of them. Never fear, they will be revealed to us — but not harshly. God's dealing with us is not always easy, but he is profoundly tender. He does not ask anything we are unable to give. This is the one process in life we can absolutely trust because God is absolutely trustworthy. We do not control this adventure — God does.

The great mystics promise that in the end, the last and most intimate vestiges of clinging to one's own interests will go. It is good to know this at the beginning. It gives us a sense of direction and enables us to cooperate as we can. If we know our selfishness must go and we have a chance to do a selfless deed or go without something we want, these efforts move us toward the goal. They cost us something, but they give us strength.

Grace for the Journey

If we "go for it" with God, will there be help along the way? Yes…more than we can ask for, more than we can dream of. God's grace for his journeying children is overwhelming. His support never pauses. In the Islamic tradition there is a saying, "If a person goes one mile toward God, God comes ten miles toward him or her." This is true. God's help comes with absolute reliability.

The spiritual life is the ultimate adventure. There are surprises around every bend. The effects of the goal itself are strewn along the pathway in small forms. We are startled by dynamic streams of peace. Joy erupts into our awareness for no particular reason.

Insights open our minds to entirely new understanding. New capacities appear within ourselves. Our prayer and contemplative practices come alive. We receive help for every concrete aspect of our lives: jobs, parenting, studies, serving, church, and relationships. All come under the scrutiny of God. Our very best is brought out by God's grace for the sake of drawing us closer to the goal of union with his heart.

Beauty and Pain

There is no limit to the beauties offered by this journey, but will there be pain too? Won't we have to suffer?

Of course — but don't we suffer anyway? Isn't there pain anyway?

When we are active on the spiritual journey, we can give our pain to God who either removes it or shows us how it can bring us closer to him. As God becomes more and more alive in our hearts, everything takes us toward our goal. Everything becomes a vehicle for his grace. Beauty and pain alike support our heart's desire and neither seems so extreme anymore.

The First Step

So we see that full union with the heart of God is the goal of this adventuresome journey. We must be ready to invest our own time and our own effort in definite daily practice. Although we know the goal will cost us our selfishness, we also know we will receive experiences that even the most clever selfishness cannot give us — fullness of joy, deep peace, flowing love, and a constant awareness of divine protection.

If all these points lead us to a more intense desire to know God directly, then we are ready to begin our journey, to say a free and happy yes to God, and to place our feet upon his path.

For Your Reflection

1. How has God's invitation come to me?
2. How have I responded to God's invitation?
3. Being realistic, how much time *could* I give to spiritual practices and prayer if I wanted to?
4. Here are Scripture passages for your consideration.

Luke 9:57-62; 14:28-31
Proverbs 3:5-6
Matthew 7:13-14
Jeremiah 29:11-14a
Psalms 27:7-10; 119:111-112
Sirach 2:1-11
Philippians 2:12-15
Deuteronomy 30:19-20a

CHAPTER FOUR

Self-knowledge:
Our Pathway
to God

The spiritual journey is unique for each person, since it is individually directed by the Holy Spirit. Yet there is an overall pattern, traceable in everyone's experience. Part of this pattern is the Good Friday/Easter theme. That is, seen from a particular viewpoint, there is a continuous reliving of death and resurrection or self-offering and transformation. The great mystics have called the crucifixion side of the pattern the "purification" or "purgative" stage. If we think of stages, however, we are only partly accurate. Like all development, spiritual life grows a step at a time, but these steps rarely proceed in a straight line.

Healing of Wounds

The words *purification* and *purgation* seem severe to me. Somehow they sound like having one's insides washed out with gritty soap. We may have the notion that purification is mostly awful and forbidding. Such an idea may even prevent us from setting out on this most wonderful of journeys. That would be too bad because the predominant experience of many people in the cleaning-up stage is quite beautiful. Feelings of great relief accompany the process, along with much healing of old wounds and the profound comfort of fears disappearing for good.

The transformation promised in spiritual growth is real. It improves the quality of our daily experience. I used to think that the purgative stage was a matter of forcibly ridding myself of all faults and nasty habits and had to be completed before anything better could happen. But as my own journey goes on, I find myself met with unexpected compassion. There are marvels as well as corrections. I am shown that faults and nastiness are symptoms of deeper wounds. What a blessing to find that when deeper layers are healed, negative behaviors often cease of their own accord.

So it turns out that purification or purgation really means healing. Healing sometimes has painful moments, often quite intense. Because of this pain, we can compare these moments in a small way to crucifixion. However, we must fully recognize them to be the Spirit in action, bringing into our awareness what needs to be healed. If we can stay with these moments quietly, remaining aware of the experience, however sharp it seems, the unwanted traits are lifted away, usually not to return. Then God's peace can reach a new depth within us, and we are able to hold it.

Practice Self-knowledge

If we wish to cooperate with this healing, this purification, what can we do? We can practice self-knowledge. We can actively investigate ourselves and offer to God all we find, one thing at a time, for his loving, healing action. If we ask for help, the Holy Spirit will show us, one thing at a time, what needs to be opened and offered and healed.

Active self-investigation is not "examination of conscience." Self-investigation is for information, not for evaluation. Indeed, if we evaluate our findings too quickly, we might close down the process. We need to know exactly what we are like and what goes on in us. We cannot offer ourselves blindfolded. We can offer only what is clearly our very own. Therefore we must be aware of what we are. We must continuously come to know ourselves more and more completely so we can consciously offer ourselves to God's love more and more deeply.

Steps to Self-knowledge

We may practice getting to know ourselves, investigating ourselves, while we are busily involved in our lives as well as when we are quiet and reflective. For example, if you watch yourself at the breakfast table, what do you notice? If you notice, "Aha! I am sluggish at this time. That's something I didn't really see before." What else do you notice as you begin the day's work? "Oh, I notice that part of me would rather be fishing, so I have difficulty settling into the task at hand." You get the idea. Just take note of what you see. That's the first step.

As a second step, we can deepen our practice by observing how the noticed trait functions in us. We may discover that when we feel sluggish, we tend to be short-tempered or, perhaps, more gentle. We may see that a divided mind does not serve us well; it neither helps with the task nor takes us to the lake! When we begin to learn how our habits, reactions, old tapes, and assumptions actually work inside us, we can offer to God's loving heart not only the surface of ourselves but the deeper aspects too.

We can also make special quiet times for self-investigation and reflection. If we allow ourselves to look gently within, we find that we know much more about ourselves than we may ordinarily realize. In our relaxed moments we can ask God to show us what we need to offer next. Caution: Do not ask unless you really want to see because the Spirit always answers this prayer!

Offering All to God

Whatever we find, we need not disapprove of ourselves nor feel pleased with ourselves. We accept what we find and then we offer all to God. If we offer something negative, we ask him to heal whatever underlies it. If we find something positive, we offer it to him to be used as he wills, to be changed, or whatever. When we offer God our habits, qualities, responses, we actually do give them away. They are ours no longer. They are God's. He can do whatever he wants with them.

Since God always does only what tends toward our joy, our peace, and the love that he is, most often God heals us. Healing brings freedom, strength, wonder, and an increasing sense of lightness and good humor about life. We also begin to discover — amazingly — that the faults we had taken so seriously can be whisked away with remarkable speed if we do not cling to them.

(Let's not deceive ourselves; we do indeed cling to faults and other negative parts of ourselves. That's why we must offer them to God too.)

Fringe Benefits

Fascinating side effects appear as we practice this kind of self-knowing. A particularly helpful one is the improved quality of our attention. If we think a moment, we know that we do not always give full and loving attention to the moment at hand. We often do not concentrate completely or for very long. We are planning the future or remembering the past. We are mentally busy elsewhere and only mechanically present. How often in conversation do we say yes, only to realize a few minutes later that we have no memory of what we said yes to?

As we practice attending to ourselves for the sake of self-knowledge, our attention is strengthened. A strong capacity for attention is important. We need it for good relationships, we need it for accomplishment of any task, we need it for deeper prayer, we need it to know God.

Deeper self-knowledge increases our attentiveness. In turn, deeper attentiveness supports our self-awareness. We find ourselves more often aware of what is going on within us at the moment it is happening rather than later by recall. As our ability to pay attention increases, we can remember God more constantly, no matter what we are doing or feeling. In time we will become fully involved in our living and, at the same time, fully attentive to God within our hearts. We may laugh or cry or work or play, all before the face of God in our hearts. Then our self-knowledge and self-offering go on in the very midst of all our activities and concerns. We discover that God is never absent — we were the absent ones.

Transformation Begins

As we know ourselves better and offer ourselves more and more to the compassionate heart of God, we are gradually changed. At some point we begin to feel like new persons. The holy transformation has begun, and we have become aware of it. We may look back over a year or two and realize that our habitual feeling-tone is not the same. The new is better. We may not behave or react in the same old familiar ways. We like the new ways better. Brand-new, unexpected experiences come. In fact, we may feel so different that all experiences seem new.

These realizations are like little Easters scattered through our daily lives. Something has died, yes, and something else has arisen in us. When Jesus was crucified, he fully experienced death. When he was resurrected, his whole human self was transformed — so much so that his disciples had difficulty recognizing him when they saw him again.

So we see how the Christian spiritual journey can be viewed as a constant reliving of Good Friday and Easter, but in small scale. That in us which is less than Christ is healed out of us; that in us which is worthy is increased. All is offered to God so all is transformed, a little at a time. One thing at a time is crucified, and it may or may not be painful at the moment. Then one thing at a time is resurrected, reborn, transformed into something new. Bit by bit, we actually become the "new creation" that was and is Jesus' intention for all.

Our active effort in this transformation may take many forms, including getting to know how we really are, so we can offer ourselves to God in full awareness, so he in turn can make us new. At the end of our spiritual journey, we will be totally new, one with Christ. That is our eternal Easter.

For Your Reflection

1. In what areas do I need healing? In which do I feel no need for change?
2. Make a list titled: "Patterns I have seen in myself." (Remember — no evaluations!)
3. When and for how long am I truly attentive to myself?
4. Here are Scripture passages that may help in the quest for self-knowledge.

   Galatians 5:16-26
   1 John 1:8-9; 3:1-3
   Sirach 11:20-28
   Matthew 13:24-30; 25:1-13
   1 Timothy 4:6-12
   Luke 21:34-36
   Psalms 19:8-15; 51:9-14; 141:1-5
   2 Corinthians 5:17

CHAPTER FIVE

A Stillness
Filled With God

When we have said a well-considered yes to God's invitation to the journey into his heart, we naturally want to find the best way to cooperate with his new activity within us. While the form of the journey will be unique to each of us, there are experiences common to all the great mystics.

Perhaps the most universal of these experiences is the daily practice of contemplation. This is the central effort, the key spiritual discipline. Some even insist that daily contemplative prayer is the only absolutely indispensable discipline.

Some may consider contemplative prayer a special gift reserved for the great saints. But contemplative practice is the best path to a close relationship with God. And it is available to all who wish to deepen their heart's journey into God.

Opening to God

Contemplation has been variously defined. It has been called a "long, loving look at God" by some. Today many call it "centering prayer." While it is sometimes called meditation, in Christianity meditation usually refers to "thinking about" God, which is quite different from contemplation.

The practice of contemplation takes place in solitude and quiet, when our whole being — body, mind, emotions, soul — opens to God. This is not the time to make resolutions or ponder Scripture or to think about anything. Contemplation is opening our total selves in loving stillness to the Spirit of God.

For some, stillness seems almost impossible. Others take to it immediately and wholly. For most, it is a challenging practice in which God gradually reveals himself to us. However awkward it may seem, we can at least begin. Everything else we need will be granted to us by God.

Enter the Quiet Place

The external part of the practice is simple enough. First we choose a time when we can be alert and a place where we can be quiet and alone. Then we go there — every day. We take a relaxed physical position, keeping our body comfortable, our spine straight. (A straight spine supports the body so we are less likely to squirm.)

Next we turn our attention within ourselves. We may focus on the space where our heart is located. To help the mind become quiet, we can follow (but not change or control) our breathing. Or we can repeat silently a chosen prayer phrase or a word. Some well-used prayer phrases include "Jesus Christ, Son of God, have mercy on me" (known as the Jesus Prayer) or simply "Jesus, mercy." A single word also may be chosen like "love" or "God" or "shalom" or simply the name "Jesus."

Whether we enter contemplation by following our breathing or by selecting a prayer phrase or a word, our method should have the following characteristics:

- It should be simple. Complicated methods or prayers are not apt to help us be quiet.
- It should be consistent, something we can stay with over a long period. Experimenting at the beginning is fine, but we need to be consistent for real depth to open in us.
- It should be attractive to us. We will not stay with something we do not find engaging.
- It should be positive. Whatever we repeat in our minds will enter deeply into our consciousness, so we must choose a word we *want* to abide within us.

When we have followed our breathing or repeated our prayer phrase for our chosen period of time, we gradually open our eyes and return our awareness to the room. We always finish by giving heartfelt thanks to God for our period of prayer.

This Vast Silence

We do not reproach ourselves when thoughts distract us. We simply return our attention to the word or the breath. If emotions arise, the best way to quiet them is to watch them and let them come. If we do not get involved in them, they will fall away of their own accord. When our body, thoughts, and emotions have become stilled, we will experience a deep serenity. This vast silence, this quiet loving, is God. Our simple, uninterrupted loving attention to that silence is contemplation.

The practice is not easy. Our habits are busy, noisy, and very stubborn. Only bit by bit do we approach this great silence. Only bit by bit does love appear within us. At first it may be the flash of a moment. Later our minds may remain focused on love for a few seconds. Gradually, with consistent practice, deeper experiences come. The Spirit knows precisely how much we can receive and hold, and he will give us just that much. Whether it is a flash, a few moments, or longer, the experience of God is always characterized by love and the joy that goes with love.

Sometimes we may think nothing has happened. Sometimes we may have recognizable, even dramatic, episodes. Many of us simply and beautifully feel quiet, profoundly peaceful and joyful. Most often love enters our awareness, but sometimes there is pain. This, too, is for growth. We need not be afraid.

Whatever happens, we should not cling to the experience. We are on a journey. We appreciate each scene as it appears to us but keep walking toward the goal — God himself. Probably each practice period will be different. One thing we can be sure of — not one is wasted. The Holy Spirit is alert to our efforts and is active within us whether or not we recognize his presence.

Contemplation is most effective when practiced daily. I tried for a long time to avoid that principle. Five days a week, I thought. Or every other day. I practiced each way for months, then suddenly knew it must be every day. Shortly after I began to practice daily contemplation, the quality of my journey changed. In a year I felt for the first time that my journey was fully under way. Others have had similar experiences.

God's Gift of Grace

There is a possible pitfall in speaking of this as "practice." It is the somewhat subtle idea that if we practice enough, we can achieve the desired result. But contemplation of God is not an achievement. As long as we think of it as a skill we learn or a state we produce, we cling too tightly to ourselves. *We* do not *do it* — God gives it. It is grace. We practice to be open to receive the gift, but it will be given when God wills. Most of us need to practice letting go because it is not a familiar condition in our lives.

Contemplation of God is an experience we can all desire and

seek, pray for and practice toward. In fact, without wanting it and praying for it, it is unlikely we will receive it. Without actively seeking it, it is unlikely we will receive it. Without practice, we will not hold it for long.

Embracing the Whole

If we practice self-knowledge along with daily contemplation, we will see that our quiet time is affected by other aspects of our life. For example, if I go to a movie in the evening, my early morning contemplation will likely turn into a rerun. Does that mean the movie is a sin or I should never go to a movie? No. It means I have choices. Which is more important to me? Can adjustments be made? For me, the adjustment was to go to the movies in the afternoon so I can rerun the movie on the same day. Then my morning contemplative practice is not invaded.

We will also begin to notice negative feelings and behavior, like anger or discourtesy. These may seem especially strong, not because they become stronger with contemplative practice, but because we become more sensitive to them. We may also discover a few unappealing characteristics we hadn't noticed before.

Our first tendency when this happens is to berate ourselves or fear for ourselves or get discouraged. But all the great spiritual directors urge us to rejoice! Why? Because once we have seen something, we can offer it to God for healing. Our purification has begun and *that* is indeed cause for rejoicing. We are on our way home.

When something in our living does not support our contemplative practice, we must decide how to respond. In the beginning such a decision may stretch us a little. But in time our prayer becomes so unspeakably important that when something gets in the way, we are glad to let it go, to change it, to uproot it, or to beg God to heal it.

There are also practices we can build into our living to actively support our contemplation and fit us to receive God's fullness in our lives. They enhance our contemplative practice and are themselves beautifully rewarding. Some of these are discussed in the following chapters.

For Your Reflection

1. Is contemplative prayer at all attractive to me?
2. Do I seek certain kinds of inner experiences? What kinds?
3. What activities in my life do I already recognize as *not* supportive of deeper prayer? Do I want to continue with these?
4. Here are scriptural passages to accompany your practice of contemplation.

Psalms 1:1-3; 27:4; 63:1-9; 119:10-16
Sirach 50:28-29
Colossians 4:2
Jude 1:20-21
Matthew 6:6; 13:44-47
Romans 8:26-27
Luke 2:19

CHAPTER SIX

The Power of a
Well-trained Will

Will power. Most of us have such a low opinion of our own will, we fail to recognize its potential. The force of steadily exerted will power has saved lives, made athletes of disabled people, changed nations, and made ordinary persons into saints. Christian spiritual writings throughout history insist that the condition of the will is the key to the journey to God.

A strong will creates circumstances according to the direction it flows. A weak will simply gives in to momentary desires. Our lives are pervaded by our likes and dislikes, our wants and repulsions. These emotions control our choices and our behavior. We know from experience how hard it is to refuse ourselves what we desire. While a will that is trained and turned toward God is our powerful ally, an untrained will makes the journey to God almost impossible.

Following our will is like driving a team of horses. If the driver can control them, they will take him precisely where he wants to go. If the driver is not firm, the horses go where they wish and simply take the driver along. Our desires are like horses — the hand on the reins is our will.

Why have Christian saints always valued the human will so highly? In our Christian tradition the will is the part of the human being that has the capacity to receive and give love. Love is more than an emotion, and love goes beyond romance. Love is eternal; it is God himself. For that divine quality of love, the will is uniquely fitted.

Choosing Wisely

The masters of the Christian spiritual life know that eternal love is rooted in our ability to choose well. As the Marriage Encounter program teaches, love is not a feeling, it is a decision. The will has the potential to receive divine love, which can direct our attention and hold it in our chosen path.

The person whose will has the power to turn toward God and remain turned toward him is the one who will be able to receive divine love and give it back to God and to the world. In this mysterious receiving and giving, God who is love dwells in the will. This only becomes possible, however, when the will has been trained to receive God.

We need to be able to choose whatever will help us on our journey and to act on that choice. We need to be alert to the interior hints of the Spirit and strong to respond cooperatively.

We know our difficulty. Let us say that we fully understand the importance of getting up a little earlier to practice centering prayer. But when the alarm rings at 5:30 a.m., our clarity is submerged in our desire to enjoy the easy, delicious warmth for another half hour.

Our will must awaken at the same time we do or our prayer will be put off for another day.

If our will has been sleeping most of our life, it is not likely to begin awakening just because we have a new idea. We have to train our will to help us. A quarterback throws thousands of passes to train his arm and eye to throw well at the critical moment. So, too, we have to train our will to be ready to cooperate with the Spirit when it acts in us.

A Strong, Steady Will

The will needs two characteristics. It must be strong and it must be steady. Neither the weak nor the fickle can live fully in God. If we are weak, we allow our desires to create our life and make our choices. If we are fickle, one day we live for our possessions and the next we think it would be nice to love God — and we do not grow. If, however, the will is strong, we will be able to choose the good and act on it. If the will is steady, we can keep on acting on our good choices.

A strong and steadfast will can be acquired with training, and as with any training, we must begin small. At the end of a long retreat, our retreat master cautioned us against making big resolutions like "From now on I will get up every morning to pray." We are deceiving ourselves with this kind of thinking. But we can decide to get up early *tomorrow* morning. In the beginning we choose little things that succeed and gradually increase to the strength and steadiness we seek.

Training Exercises

The first principle in training the will is this: deliberately but cheerfully go against our desires.

We may choose to do something we don't like to do or refuse to do something we like. These efforts are experiments, chosen for practice only. The specific choices are not important in themselves. We may choose to eat something we don't like or say no to something we crave. We may sit in an uncomfortable chair or park a couple of blocks away from our destination. These are all exercises to strengthen the will, invented merely for training.

We can also use our duties as training exercises by changing our attitude toward them. A necessary task that we may not like can be accomplished for the sake of our journey. If there is something we desire, we can let it go for God.

It is good to practice playfully, as if it were a game. We can say to ourselves, "Let's see if I *can* do this!" A playful attitude works out well. The very lightheartedness of it makes growth easier.

As we practice with small desires, we begin to discover a tiny but definite sense of new power. We are calling forth the beginnings of a great but neglected force — and our will responds to a playful, gentle touch.

We can also train the will by watching our desires, likes, and dislikes instead of mindlessly doing what they prompt us to do. As we watch them, a curious thing happens — they change of themselves. Our desires are seldom strong in themselves. They only seem strong because we catered to them for so long.

An interesting exercise is to window-shop at stores that interest you. Remember, you are not going to buy but to practice watching your desires fluctuate. As you stroll down the mall, keep your inner eye open and observe what goes on inside you. This is such a revealing practice that I won't even try to predict your discoveries.

Focusing on the Goal

You can also strengthen your will by focusing on your goal. When this journey was begun, you gave considerable thought to the direction you were taking. Your plan was to move closer and closer to God until you came to live completely in his heart.

Each morning, as early as possible, take a few moments to recall the goal. It is best to do this before getting out of bed, but whenever you remember, you can pause and give attention to your journey for a few moments. The memory of the goal intensifies motivation and strengthens the will.

As you go through your day, you ask of each activity and decision, "Does this serve my goal well? Does it move me toward God?" Often this question alone is enough to support the will. Gradually, you lose interest in desires that do not serve you well.

This practice also helps to create a steadfast will. The long-distance runner knows where the finish line is and remains attentive to it throughout the long effort. That focus keeps him or her going. Saint Paul said it well: "I continue my pursuit toward the goal, the prize of God's upward calling, in Christ Jesus. Let us, then, who are 'perfectly mature' adopt this attitude. And if you have a different attitude, this too God will reveal to you. Only, with regard to what we have attained, continue on the same course" (Philippians 3:14-16).

It is a long journey we have undertaken. We have seen that there will be help along the way, but we must keep going, our hearts full of willing perseverance. For that end, keeping the goal in focus is a great help.

Practice, Practice, Practice

No matter which exercise we use to train our will, we must practice it every day. My piano teacher always said that fifteen minutes of practice every day was more effective than an hour every other day. So it is with any training program.

As the will grows stronger and becomes steadier, we experience a wonderful new sense of freedom. We begin to choose wisely and to act consistently on our choices. This freedom is delightful, better than a myriad of pleasures. A strong will is a free will — free to receive infinite love and to become truly the inner dwelling of the

Father. No longer do we feel trapped by petty desires that distract our direction. As the will increases in strength and steadiness, our happiness grows until we experience a steady, peace-filled determination.

For Your Reflection

1. What little thing that I dislike shall I do as a practice this week?
2. What are my attitudes now toward my duties?
3. Through one whole day, how does each activity affect my spiritual life? Does it serve me well?
4. What is the result of carrying out the first question?
5. Here are Scripture passages that may help in training the will.

Matthew 16:24-27; 26:40-46
Proverbs 5:22-23; 6:23
Wisdom 6:17-19
Romans 7:20-25a
2 Timothy 1:7; 2:1
Ephesians 3:14-20; 6:10
Philippians 4:11-13
Hebrews 12:5-13
Joshua 1:7-9
Sirach 2:1-9; 32:14
1 Corinthians 9:25-27; 15:58

CHAPTER SEVEN

The Human Heart
Is Made for Goodness

All of us want to be good. We may be confused about what goodness is, we may not think goodness is possible for us, and we may act in not-so-good ways sometimes — but the human heart is made for goodness, and one way or another everyone wants it.

This fact gives us a head start in our inward journey into God. At our deepest we already wish to become virtuous and noble and compassionate. To this end we are urged by the Church to practice virtue, to cultivate virtuous behavior. We are taught to be kind, to obey the commandments, and to pray. We begin by doing good deeds and by trying to make moral decisions. For those consciously desiring union with God, however, the practice of virtue is much more.

God's Gift of Self

We usually think of a virtue as a quality we can possess. Early Christian writers had a more profound view. They said the essence of virtue is God's own qualities hidden in human action or attitude. Virtue belongs essentially to God. Growth in virtue depends on the grace of God as well as on human effort. We practice a virtue until our heart opens enough to receive the essence of that virtue, which is the corresponding quality of God. This is God giving himself. It has even been called a continuation of the Incarnation, since in it God acts in human life.

For us, virtue begins as a practice and ends as a permanent part of our character, established in us by God. Gradually, God makes us like himself by giving us his own qualities. The more virtuous we are, the more like God we are. The more we are like God, the closer we are to divine union with him. The practice of virtue is a powerful effort to become more like God.

Defining Virtues

What are virtues? Lists vary as widely as their authors. Most familiar are probably the four cardinal virtues listed by Plato: justice, prudence, temperance, and fortitude. To these Christianity adds the three theological virtues: faith, hope, and love. But every writer on the spiritual life suggests a somewhat different grouping, although all place love at the top. Saint Maximus the Confessor said the four basics are moral judgment, justice, courage, and self-restraint, which lead to wisdom and meekness. Saint Mark the Ascetic lists long-suffering, humility, vigilance, and self-control. Diadochos of Photiki includes moderation in eating, humility, patience, chastity, and obedience. Saint Gregory Nazianzen lists discretion, understanding, courage, charity, and justice, which balances all the rest. One saintly writer goes on for a full page and a half with his list of virtues!

A common way to organize the virtues is to divide them into those that are good for the body and those that are good for the soul. For the body, the virtues are mostly ascetic practices like fasting or taxing the body as well as service to others and self-supporting labor. For our more inner aspects, Maximus suggests these: for the mind, spiritual reading, meditation, and prayer; for the emotions, spiritual love and longing for God; and for the desires, moderation and self-control.

A Circle of Love

All virtues are transformations. They do not come from thinking about them or from understanding them mentally. It is not enough to admire them, nor are they automatic in Christian life. If we seek spiritual progress, we must begin quite practically to become more virtuous within ourselves and in our actions. We need to practice, for the practice of any one virtue leads eventually to the practice of all the others.

Virtues are interdependent. We may enter their circle at any point and keep going until all have been reached. The virtues return us to a state where we can perceive the real truth of living, where we are no longer confused about goodness, and where we can experience a deep relationship with God. Most importantly, the practice of the virtues culminates in love, divine love mutually given and received.

Fringe Benefits

As we practice the virtues with this goal firmly in mind, wonderful by-products appear. The first is strength. A person who can be honest when loss may result is a strong person. One who can act wisely and courageously at great risk is a strong person. One who can forgive a vicious word or a theft is strong. It is this kind of strength that the virtues produce in us.

Another benefit of the virtues is deep serenity. Virtue is a calm, confident position. When we are clearly aware of the *quality* of decision and action we want — and virtues are mostly a matter of quality — then we know how to respond in any circumstances. We are no longer driven by fears and angers and me-first striving. When the virtues bear this fruit, we "practice, speak, hear, and think nothing but peace," says Maximus *(The Philokalia II).*

Further, the virtues support our contemplation. In fact, virtue is incomplete unless we also practice contemplation. They belong together. The peaceful fruit of virtue quiets us so much that contemplation becomes noticeably easier and deeper. Virtues also tend to unify and balance our being and center us on God. This focus also enhances our contemplation.

Subtle Traps

As we practice virtues, one caution needs to be kept firmly in mind — our motivation for this practice makes a huge difference. The saints say the only safe and legitimate reason for seeking virtue is a desire for union with God. We sometimes want virtue for lesser reasons: so we can be approved of or even admired by other people; so we can applaud ourselves for our good behavior; to acquire personal power or win merit for ourselves. Obviously, each of these motives entraps us in selfishness and pride, the exact opposite of spiritual benefit.

These lesser motives may seem easily avoidable in the beginning, but they can sneak in subtly. For example, a man may begin practicing honesty and then discover that a store has made a large error in his favor. Of course, the practitioner of honesty makes it known and pays what is due. Then the clerk heaps praise on him, and he leaves the store feeling quite grand, quite proud, of his virtue. Watch out! Does feeling grand like this lead to God?

The best way to avoid these subtle traps, say the saints, is always to remember that God alone gives us the grace to be virtuous. We may practice, but real virtue is God's transformation in us. The only genuine response to that gift is gratitude. So when we are able to act virtuously or to experience a virtuous attitude, it's best to thank the Source of all virtue. Thanksgiving is always true, and it keeps us humble when we recall that only God makes us good.

A Chance to Learn

Another caution for us moderns is our tendency to see everything as a moral matter. It is vital for our psychological health that we practice virtues *as a practice* and not as a heavy moral demand. For example, suppose we are practicing non-stealing, which means not *ever* taking anything that is not ours. We see a ten-dollar bill lying on the street. Do we pocket it? If this is a moral question, there is nothing wrong with taking the money. There is no way to return it to the owner and, after all, we found it.

But if we are sincere about our spiritual practice as practice, we do not pocket the bill. Why? Simply because it does not belong to us. It is a good chance to practice, so we leave it alone. (Incidentally, the amount of resistance we feel to this idea might say something about our subtle involvement in greed!)

Interesting, yes?

Practicing virtues also means we are not hard on ourselves when we fail in a particular instance. The effort to cooperate in our own transformation can lead to a case of scruples if not handled lightly. Almost everything in our life presents an opportunity for practice if we wish to take it as such. But we might also drive ourselves terribly if we feel obligated to be "at it" every moment. In the long run consistency will be important, but along the way practice is simply practice. It is a light and cheerful experiment, a free chance to learn.

Getting Started

To begin our practice we choose a single virtue, one that appeals to us and that we have a chance of doing well. The "big ones" like love should be left until later. We should start with whatever good quality seems interesting and desirable right now.

First, we ponder it. What exactly is this quality? What does it feel like? How does it express itself in behavior? What is the nature of this virtue? We ask other people what it means to them. We look it up in the writings on spiritual life.

Next, we pray for this virtue. "Prayer is the mother of all virtues," someone has said. We ask God for insight about how to practice and for his gift of our chosen virtue. We ask him to provide opportunities for practice. And we thank him even for our interest in the practice of virtue! It, too, is his gift.

Continuing to practice means being alert to chances to act on our chosen virtue. We must be attentive during the day. The opportunities will be there, probably more than we expected. We must use them and observe our own inner responses. Most of all, we must keep gratitude foremost.

And we can be encouraged by the words of Saint John Damascene: "Truly blessed is the one who seeks virtue and pursues it and inquires diligently into its nature, since it is through virtue that we approach God and enter into spiritual communion with him" (*The Philokalia*).

(*The two quotations and most of the other references in this chapter are taken from* THE PHILOKALIA, *translated and edited by G.E.H. Palmer, Philip Sherrard, and Kallistos Ware, Volume I [Faber and Faber, Inc.].*)

For Your Reflection

1. What virtues are already mine?
2. What virtues would I like to cultivate?

3. What virtue shall I practice for this week?
4. *(At the end of the week.)* What has been the result of the third question?
5. Here are Scripture passages for your support.

   Galatians 5:19-26; 6:7-10
   Colossians 3:12-17
   James 1:22-26
   Ephesians 5:8-10
   Micah 6:8
   Sirach 17:17-20; 18:7-13
   Luke 6:43-45
   Romans 5:3-5
   Proverbs 11

6. Look up the virtues that interest you by name in a concordance. Then read the Bible references given there.

CHAPTER EIGHT

The Practice
of Not Stealing

An interesting virtue to practice is inner obedience to the seventh commandment: You shall not steal (mentioned as an example in the last chapter). Why should we need *practice* in this commandment? We are not thieves, are we?

No, we are not, as long as we think of stealing at the level of legality or ordinary morality. But we are not speaking here of sin or morality. We are on an inward journey to become closer to God. When we consider non-stealing from the point of view of our highest goal, union with God in love, then it is different.

Not to steal, seen from this spiritual perspective, means to take nothing for ourselves that does not belong to us, nothing at all. Like most practices we begin with the obvious. In time the practice itself will lead us to subtleties and strengthen us where we need it.

Moreover, this virtue melts into other virtues, so no matter where we begin, we are drawn into the same depths.

Look at Ourselves

First, we must take a good look at ourselves. Do we take anything that is not ours? For example, do we taste food at the produce counter? Do we copy tapes or videos instead of buying them, thus stealing from the author and the producer? Do we cheat a little on our taxes? Do we take credit for ideas that someone else originated? Do we loaf on company time or use company resources for personal purposes? Do we borrow without informing or asking? Do we fail to return books that we have borrowed?

The selfish part of us is prone to respond, "But those things are so small! It doesn't matter to the company if I make a few copies or to the grocer if I taste a grape!" That is true. That's exactly the difference between the legal point of view and an interior point of view. We do not undertake a particular spiritual practice for the sake of others who may or may not be affected by it. We do not practice a virtue because of morality or rules. Our practice aims for total cooperation in the purification of our own spirit so God may dwell more fully in us. If that seems extreme to others, whose goals are less than God himself, then so be it.

We do need to keep our own motivation of holy cooperation clear. If we try to practice this virtue zealously for habitual, moral reasons, we can fall into miserable feelings of guilt. These are not necessary but follow upon inadequate motivation. This can happen in all spiritual practices. It's good to remember that we are not being judged for the morality or righteousness of our practice. We are working to perfect a virtue solely for the sake of drawing closer to God.

When considering whether we steal or not, we easily recognize that almost everyone steals at these smaller, less obvious levels. Small stealing and big stealing have this in common: stealing is grasping for things, for life's rewards, even for life itself. It is our ego-centered self claiming everything it can reach.

A friend and I began this practice at the same time. I recall walking down a neighborhood street and coming across a couple of big bolts in the middle of the road. Normally, I would have pocketed them "in case I can use them some day." This time I laughingly left them there.

An odd thing happened next. I felt as if a weight had been lifted; I felt lighter. It was subtle. If I had not been paying attention inwardly, I might not have noticed it. Yet something was different in my heart. I called my friend to see how she was faring. She reported an identical experience, though it was a quarter she had seen and left on a sidewalk.

How This Practice Helps Us

How does this practice of non-stealing help us? First, not taking what is not ours will illuminate our own acquisitiveness. The example mentioned in Chapter Seven is excellent. If I see a ten-dollar bill lying in the street, what does it cost me to leave it there? Mentally, an argument ensues: "Why shouldn't I have it? I can't return it to the owner; who knows who lost it? If I don't pick it up, someone else surely will, and I need it for....Besides, finders keepers, right?"

What is the motive beneath this mental quarrel? Isn't it acquisitiveness? This is most obvious where cash is involved. Acquisitiveness is a name for a particular kind of ego-centered attitude. A less fancy word is greed. Our ego feeds on getting, having, and owning. It says "mine" and "keep" a lot. That attitude holds us at a distance from God.

Further, non-stealing gives us a clearer awareness of our true position in our world. As we refrain from taking what is not ours, we recognize that we occupy a certain place, and that place has limits. That is good for us to know, as it helps us accept our life more fully, more appreciatively, more humbly. If we find it hard to accept our place, then this practice will expose a certain ambition in us, not necessarily a healthy ambition from the viewpoint of spiritual growth.

There is an almost poignant honesty about ourselves in this practice. It is like humility. We become increasingly willing to let ourselves have what we have, be what we are, without comparing ourselves to others and without constantly gazing over the fences of our own space in life. This is one beautiful fruit of this practice. It becomes, with time and attention, less the practice of *not* stealing and more the practice of *quiet acceptance.*

We may experience a taste of personal dignity. This dignity does not come from recognition because a practice like non-stealing is not usually visible to others. The dignity belongs to the image of God within us. It is natural to us, but we rarely experience it because we are not open enough. The practice of non-stealing opens us to our own natural dignity.

Years ago an acquaintance told of sitting on a step along a busy street on a chilly day. A bent, beaten-looking man came by and asked my friend if he had an extra pair of socks. Wordlessly, my acquaintance began to take off his shoes to give the man the socks he had on. The beaten-looking man stood up a little straighter and said, "No, mister. I do not want *your* socks." He walked away, erect.

When we stand for purest integrity by avoiding every taint of stealing, in that very moment we taste what it means to be fully human, as God intends us to be. That fullness allows us to accept ourselves and our circumstances even more freely. Little by little we find that we do not need to grasp at life, we do not need to be on constant alert to grab whatever we can. We may find that we actually already have enough and more. Contentment begins to flow quietly into a heart that has long been grabby. Contentment leads to peace, and where there is true peace, God is found.

The practice of not stealing even the smallest, most subtle thing requires vigilance, itself a singularly valuable spiritual trait. It also requires self-restraint, a direct reduction of the ego's power in our living. Such reduction is the very best contribution we can make toward cooperation with the Holy Spirit, because the instant we set aside a bit of our ego-centeredness, the Spirit fills that space if we ask for it.

Does non-stealing mean we become passive toward our lives, not giving effort to that home we dream of or to an education we seek or to reliable transportation we need? I do not think so. Non-stealing is not the same as refusing to earn. Working to be able to buy what we want is not a hindrance to loving God deeply. We must work; we cannot, with integrity, take what we have not earned, even the least thing. That is exactly the practice.

A Refusal to Manipulate

At more subtle levels, the practice of non-stealing involves a refusal to manipulate other people in any way, which is a good idea in itself! When we flatter another or threaten another, when we relate to another expecting a certain return, we are really *stealing* emotionally. That is, one is trying to grab certain responses like approval or particular efforts or favors. It is possible to manipulate some people so as to evoke the response we want, but the favor is not freely given. We have subtly stolen it by emotional pressure.

Any *use* of other people is essentially the same theft. The practice of non-stealing in emotional areas requires a very caring attention to the way we relate to other people. Some of us tend to use those closest to us; others tend to manipulate strangers or business acquaintances. It does not matter whom we use. It is all emotional, personal theft.

As one practices non-stealing by leaving the money where it is, by watching our relationships, by leaving everything alone that is not ours, we slowly find that the grip of greed (material or emotional) on the heart is loosened. An inner tightness begins to relax.

The heart eases and opens. When that happens, God is right there to fill it with his own heart.

As we accept what life has allotted us, even just a little, a mysterious alchemy happens in our spirit. We become more of what we most truly, most deeply, most wonderfully, are — born for deepest communion with God.

In this state, free of grasping, gratitude arises in the heart. What began as a definite practice, an effort, to avoid claiming for ourselves what is not ours evolves into an inner freedom filled with spontaneous thanksgiving. That is grace. It is a common experience in spiritual practices. We begin with our own efforts but end with freedom and peace and God's love, given to our innermost self. The practice becomes the goal; it has prepared us to receive God in more fullness, as God so fully wants to give himself.

For Your Reflection

1. In what ways do I perhaps steal?
2. What are my own attitudes about my stealing? Is it acceptable? Does it serve me well? Why or why not?
3. Do I manipulate people? How? What attitude is to be found here?
4. Following are Scripture passages for your thoughts.

   Exodus 20:15
   1 Thessalonians 4:9-12
   Proverbs 2:9-10; 14:16; 19:1; 21:6; 28:24; 29:24; 30:7-9
   Sirach 2:6; 4:1-6, 31; 6:1-4; 7:32-33; 29:23; 31:8-10
   Acts 4:32-35
   Galatians 6:7-9

CHAPTER NINE

Handling
the Inner Obstacles

S omeone has said — was it Pogo? — "We have met the enemy
and it is us."

At the right moment in our spiritual growth, each of us
makes the same discovery. The biggest obstacles to divine life are
not circumstances at all but parts of ourselves. By the grace of God,
that discovery is repeated again and again. It is a great gift if it stays
fresh within us because it keeps us alert.

The first time we see it clearly can be a shock. I can remember
driving along an empty freeway, thinking about an earlier conversation. A teacher I profoundly respected had asked me an embar-
rassing question, so I lied to him. The question was of no real
importance. All the more was I stung when I faced what I had done.
It was as if all my faults stood up before me. Hundreds of little

dishonesties, thousands of small resentments, countless fears, more and more paraded before my shocked awareness. I felt shaken, ashamed. All I wanted, I always told myself, was God. Yet all these barriers thrived in me, and I had not even seen them clearly. Indeed, the enemy of my deepest goal was — and is — myself.

When this happens, the only sane thing is to cry out to God for help. God is faithful. The Spirit will respond in exactly the way we need. Maybe we will burn hotter and longer. Maybe peace will come. Maybe more obstacles will be shown us. Maybe we will be given inklings of how to work against these obstacles to our goal. God's response may come immediately or in driblets over a long time; maybe both. We need never fear that we face our enemies and obstacles alone. We *never* do. God is *always* present to us.

However it happens to us, we are startled into unmistakable awareness that we must learn to deal with our negative emotions and nasty habits.

Handling the Obstacles

The first, but most subtle, step is to ponder the fact that these obstacles — fear, anger, inferiority, self-pity, generalized guilt, pride, lying, and all the rest — are *not* our essential self. Our essential self is always and only the image of God deep in our being. We are intensely identified with almost every other aspect of ourselves, our emotions perhaps first, but also our thinking, our bodies, and our positions in the world. We assume that all this is our real self.

Yet we know, when we attend to ourselves, that fear is an emotion that occurs within us. We are not that fear, though sometimes it may seem so. We are not our resentments nor any of the other obstacles within. All these are obstacles in our being that get in the way of our radiating forth fully the image of God. Our identification with these emotions, the feeling that we *are* what we feel limits God's dwelling within us. We cannot wrench this identification out of our perspective directly. All our spiritual practices are required, plus the ever-present grace of God.

At the beginning we can help ourselves by simply pondering this identification with our emotions and watching ourselves live our lives to notice it more.

How can we actively reduce the power of our negative emotions and habits? Anyone who has tried knows that one thing does *not* work: we cannot promise ourselves never to feel those feelings again. Without question, we will feel them again, over and over.

We begin by observing them. (Please look again at Chapter Four on self-knowledge.) When an emotion like resentment wells up in us, we can practice putting a clamp on our mouth and refusing to decide for a little while in order to *see* what is happening. This small inner distance from the emotion withdraws a bit of our identification with it and saps its power over us.

Furthermore, we can watch that emotion rampage. Stare at it! This can turn out to be genuinely funny, and a good laugh at ourselves is a wonderful spiritual help.

Then we can adopt a new practice. We can practice not allowing the negative emotion to make decisions for us. Remember that we cannot change our inner habits by direct resolution, but they will change by practice.

Here is another personal example. (I've practiced it a lot because I have so many negatives inside!) For most of my five decades of life, I have been scared. The gamut of intensity has existed, from apprehension to terror. You name it; I have been afraid of it. When I would read in the Bible "do not be afraid," it was like looking at a stone wall, virtually impossible.

Eventually, I got tired of being scared and saw what a huge obstacle fear was. So I began to observe it and practice not letting my fear make decisions for me. Once my husband and I were hiking in Zion National Park. We were headed for an enormous rock outcropping that promised a wonderful view. We paused to rest, and I saw that the trail was leading up a narrow slope with steep cliffs falling away on both sides. Terror invaded me like lightning. For a few minutes I could feel nothing but the fear. Then, by God's mercy, I saw how scared I was feeling — that small essential distance. Instantly, I knew I would walk that narrow path, scared or not, as much to defy the fear as to enjoy the view. Off I went, finding little jokes to make out loud along the way to encourage myself.

That is another way to practice against our negatives — use humor. Once I saw a young woman of tiny physique with a phobia about heights overcome her fear in one stroke with humor. She was standing on a high platform, in a perfectly safe harness. Her assignment was to jump and let herself be caught. She was paralyzed with terror, but suddenly she pounded her chest, yelled "Me, Jane!" and leaped! She was safely caught, laughing. Her phobia was broken for good.

There is a book titled *Feel the Fear...and Do It Anyway.* Precisely. The same is true for other negative emotions. Let yourself feel them, notice them, expose them, but choose to act on some other basis. For us, that other basis is a spiritual life. Our hope for life in the heart of God must be increasingly the basis of our decisions and our actions. The mystical saints testify that the emotions do not run down for many, many years. But they pass through us, ever-changing responses to life's little incidents. The more we watch them, the less power they have. The less we act on them, the weaker they become. Our hope is that one day our lives will be so filled with God's peace, God's joy, God's love, that even should such an emotion occur, it will be fleeting, like the shadow of a jet across the sun.

Positive Replacement

Another good antidote for negative thoughts and emotions sounds almost too simple, yet it is mighty. Every time we become aware of a negative thought, we can replace it deliberately with a positive one. Our ego will fight this, a sure indication that it supports our love of God.

The positive replacement need not be about the same subject. If we feel angry about something, it will not help much to tell ourselves that we really feel peaceful about it. That's a lie and compounds the difficulty. What will help is turning our attention to something we do feel good about, like the blessing of the spiritual journey or the grace of God or something very obvious like the good night's sleep we had or the pleasures of our children or friends.

The effort here is to place the power of our attention in the direction we want to move, not to allow it to circle endlessly around the obstacle we wish to avoid. Our attention always binds us to the object of our focus. We can use this principle to bind ourselves to the beautiful, to everything that leads us closer to God.

Another way to handle inner obstacles is to offer them to God for his transformation and healing. Our own efforts, though necessary, are not enough to carry us beyond all obstacles. By offering them to God, we make clear to ourselves that we do not want to cling to them any longer. This is a giant step forward. Most of us do, in fact, hang on tightly to the very attitudes and emotions that most harm our spirit. A significant part of us likes being mad, doesn't want to let go of fears, and revels in self-pity. That part of us is ego. It is not God's image at all. When we let them go, we make of them a true sacrifice to the Spirit within us.

When we offer these obstacles to God, we open ourselves to the holy process of necessary purification. We can trust God to respond to these offerings with healing, in exact proportion to our letting go, to the intensity of our offering. When we cry a heartfelt "God, *please* take away this resentment. I do not want to hate. I want only you!" then God, merciful and always ready, will do just that, sometimes dramatically, sometimes gradually, but always reliably.

So "handling" the inner obstacle that is a part of ourselves is actually a process of letting that obstacle decrease under the influence of our desire for God's life and the action of the Holy Spirit. It is not something we fix, as we might solve a problem, but it is a releasing, a surrendering of inner aspects that we no longer want to keep. More and more we want to let them go because more and more we see how much they hinder our deepest desire: life in the heart of God.

For Your Reflection

1. What is the strongest inner obstacle for me?
2. In what ways do I cling to negative feelings and attitudes?
3. What repetitive obstacles can I approach with humor?
4. Here are Scripture passages for your support.

Matthew 5:21-25; 10:28-32
Ephesians 4:30-32
Luke 12:29-32
James 1:19
Psalm 27:1-3, 11-14
Proverbs 29:11
Philippians 4:4-8
Sirach 34:13-17; 30:21-25
Mark 7:20-23
John 6:18-20
1 John 3:15-18; 4:16-18

CHAPTER TEN

Forgiveness: A Decision of the Heart

Both the Mass and the New Testament say that Jesus Christ lived and died "that sins might be forgiven." If forgiveness was that important to Jesus, then surely it is not optional for Christians who seek to follow him.

Of course, we all know that, but we find forgiving difficult and feel guilty when we cannot do it. We feel "I should forgive so-and-so, but I just can't...," and then we dislike ourselves. Let's not do that. Let's work toward a better understanding of forgiveness.

Hurt and Healing

Some understand forgiveness as an act benefiting the person who has wronged us. This is not the point. According to Jesus, we forgive for our own sakes. What we give to others, we will get back from the Father: "If you forgive others their transgressions, your heavenly Father will forgive you" (Matthew 6:14) and "For as you judge, so will you be judged" (Matthew 7:2).

Jesus also warned those who do not forgive: "Then in anger his master handed him over to the torturers....So will my heavenly Father do to you, unless each of you forgives his brother from his heart" (Matthew 18:34-35). Who is this torturer? It is our own nature. When we cannot forgive, anger is kept inside. Kept anger disturbs the body and closes the heart not only against one person but against everyone and everything. It disables us in our love, even for those near and dear to us. Finally, a heart closed to others is also closed to God. Deep prayer becomes impossible. As pilgrims, our refusal to forgive sabotages our journey. To communicate with God without barriers, we must become like Jesus, and we clearly see Jesus forgiving his tormentors from the cross.

The benefits of forgiveness are simple but profound. When we forgive, our hearts are open to give and receive love with others and with God. Injuries are healed as we forgive the one who wounded us. We are delivered from old sins and we feel more nearly whole. Because we are no longer rigidly keeping anger, we become more flexible, more free. We have more zest for living, and our prayer life is no longer disturbed by resentment. Thus it is for our own growth that we learn to forgive. When we remain angry, our spiritual practices fail to bear fruit.

A Decision of the Heart

This is not about morality. Most moral theologians agree that anger is natural and we should not punish ourselves for our feelings. As an old Chinese proverb explains, "You can't keep a bird from flying over your head. You can keep it from building a nest in your hair." We can't always keep ourselves from feeling anger, but we don't have to let our anger build a nest in our hearts. Forgiveness means letting go so God's love can flow into us and through us to others, even those who have hurt us.

The choice to forgive is a decision of the heart that has nothing to do with what has been done to us and everything to do with what we want to become. When we feel an injustice is so great that forgiveness cannot be right, we need to recall the crucifixion, totally unjust and totally forgiven. We choose to practice forgiveness for the sake of our goal.

With God's grace we can decide to be what we want to be regardless of how we are treated. "Don't get mad, get even" may channel anger for some, but for our journey such an attitude is not practical and will not lead us toward God. Instead we say, "Don't stay mad, get peaceful," thus expressing what we are practicing to become. We "get peaceful" by forgiving.

Beginning Our Practice

How can we begin to practice forgiveness? First, we allow ourselves time. Like most aspects of our spiritual journey, forgiveness must be learned. Unless we have had a dramatic experience of God's forgiveness, our ability to forgive will not be a spontaneous reaction. That simply tells us that we need to begin practicing.

Second, we declare to God our willingness to learn forgiveness and ask his blessing on our effort. This is a huge step toward God, and he welcomes us as the father welcomed the prodigal son.

We need to begin small and to be realistic. We can start with the nasty words said to us recently or the unintentional hurt dealt us by gossip. If we practice by forgiving those people we already love, our love will empower our decision. Beginning with small hurts, we learn how to approach the larger ones.

We can also let go of our expectations of others. It is unrealistic to demand that others always be kind, loving, and just. Such expectations are sure to disappoint us. We all hurt one another sometime. Once we acknowledge this and relax about it, we won't be so resentful and forgiveness will flow more easily.

We can investigate our inclination to self-justification. We often hold onto anger to justify ourselves. Being angry implies we have it right and the other person has it wrong, whatever "it" may be. If we feel so insecure that we must justify ourselves by anger, we need to get help to heal that insecurity. If self-justification is only a habit, we can ask God to take it away — and he will. Then we can try hard to *allow* our fallibility. We all know we are imperfect and it scares us. We deny it in our emotions even while we admit it in words. From emotional acceptance of our fallibility comes blessed relief and healing.

Reconditioning Our Emotions

Here is a vital point: There is a difference between our will and our emotions. Forgiveness must begin as an act of our will. Because the will belongs to the spiritual part of ourselves, God recognizes and accepts our decision to forgive. However — and this is often the sticky spot — we may not feel immediate emotional change. We have all experienced this. We forgive someone, but when we see that person unexpectedly, our anger rushes up again. Our emotions may need to be reconditioned to match our decision.

But emotions come and go if they are left alone. An emotion is a natural, largely biological energy reaction. If we acknowledge the existence of anger but *do not nourish it,* it will go away again. To see this for ourselves, we can watch our emotions for a week. When anger comes up, either low-grade burn or full-blown explosion, a part of ourselves is able to observe it and watch it expand, subside, and disappear.

This may sound far-fetched, but I can assure you it works! It requires only an effort to be honest. If we deeply desire God, we must honestly observe intrusive emotions such as anger. This takes practice, but it is utterly freeing.

Why We Get Angry

We can also help ourselves by noticing closely why we get angry. There are three basic reasons for getting angry — fear, pain, and not getting our own way (which includes those times when the world doesn't go the way we think it should). We can examine the last six times we were really mad and then determine what was beneath the anger. This will help us determine which of these categories it fits into. Once we know the nature of our anger, it is easier to let it go. We can say things like "Oh, yeah, I'm angry because so-and-so scared me." Such clarity restores our perspective and allows us to stop blaming and start forgiving.

Forgiveness and Prayer

Our practice of forgiveness needs to be supported by consistent prayer — prayer for help with forgiveness, prayer to be more like Jesus, prayer to become instruments of Jesus' forgiveness of all, prayer to open our hearts so old resentments can be healed, prayer for support when we feel newly vulnerable (unprotected by our former angers), and prayer of thanksgiving that Jesus came for forgiveness of all.

When forgiveness becomes a habit deep enough, we are much lighter within. Anger eventually becomes truly fleeting and will one day vanish altogether. Happiness can flood us, peace can inhabit us. God finds more and more space in our hearts where the anger used to be. He can now fill that space with himself. That is our hope. That is our goal. That is the assurance Jesus gave us in his life and in his death — all sins are forgiven so we can live in union with the Father.

For Your Reflection

1. What kinds of events or people do I have difficulty forgiving?
2. Do I let others' actions control my emotions and attitudes? When? How? Do I want to keep doing it that way?
3. What are ten expectations I place on spouse, Church, boss, coworkers, friends?
4. Here are Scripture passages that can help in the practice of forgiveness.

   Matthew 6:14-15; 18:21-25
   Luke 6:37-38; 7:36-50; 23:33-34
   Ephesians 4:30-32
   Sirach 28:1-7
   Psalm 130
   1 John 1:5-10
   Acts 13:37-39

CHAPTER ELEVEN

Drawing Strength From Scripture

The greatest Christians, those who became wise through communion with God, have all testified to the value of Scripture in their spiritual journey. For them, the Word of God has been companion, strength, motivation, and guidance. Even though Christians do not always agree about the exact meaning of God's Word, we do find much help when we approach it with an open heart.

Scripture includes an amazing variety of materials. Foremost among these are the stories and teachings of Jesus. Stories of the early Church, the letters of Saint Paul, and other unnamed great disciples are also found in the New Testament. The Old Testament includes stories about creation, about the people of God, as well as instructions, poetry, prayers, exhortations, and even inspired teaching-fiction.

There are many levels of meaning in holy Scripture. It can be understood as history, as prophecy, as truthful mythology, as teaching, as prayer, as reflection of interior experiences and understanding, as instruction for living, and as God speaking directly to an individual heart. These levels balance and complement one another.

Usually, we are not equally comfortable with all levels of meaning, but that only suggests we will grow as we become more familiar with the book. We need to use the commentaries and study-helps so widely available today. We also need to trust our hearts and our knowledge of our faith. If we do not fully understand everything we read, it doesn't matter because no one does.

All this biblical wealth is wonderful for our interior life. Still, wealth can do a person no good unless it is applied to daily living. The leather-bound Bible on the coffee table, dusted weekly, is not enough.

Help Yourself to Scripture

The first practice necessary to draw strength and direction from Scripture is a program of regular Bible reading. I used to think it was important to approach the Bible systematically. That's true for a thorough *study* of the Bible (which is highly recommended). But for our inner journey it is vital to begin with a part of the Bible that fascinates us, that we enjoy. Students and friends of mine have started with Mark, with Genesis, with Psalms, and one even began with Leviticus.

For a while we may even go "treasure-troving" to see what we can find. Or we may follow a program already set by the Church, like the daily Mass readings or the readings in the Liturgy of the Hours. Wherever we begin, if we follow through on the questions that arise as we read, we will be led to investigate most of the Bible. *Where* we begin is less important than *that* we begin.

Through the history of the Church, daily reading (*lectio divina*) has been regarded as a necessary aid to inner prayer and growing communion with God. So to help yourself to Scripture, choose a time, a reasonably quiet, comfortable area, a place to start — and begin!

Proceed With Caution

Begin with prayer for blessing on the reading, for insight for the mind, and understanding for the heart. Read slowly, attentively. If a phrase or a word attracts you, stay with it tenderly for a while.

You may wish to set a certain amount of time to read each day, but it's better not to set a certain amount of text. There is no need to hurry. You are simply taking a few steps along your interior journey to God. Therefore, read with some attention to your own interior life.

If questions arise, welcome them. It is a sign you are alive! The Bible is not understandable at first glance. If you feel bored, don't worry. It probably only means you're in a section not suited to your present needs. (Besides, some of the Bible *is* boring.)

If you want to challenge what you read, do so. The Bible is strong enough to stand up for itself. Take seriously your feelings, questions, and challenges, and use them to motivate you to study more deeply. Get other books, find classes (beg for them in your parish), and seek others who read the Scriptures regularly.

Christian community is vital to the deepening of our scriptural understanding and appreciation.

Over time you will become familiar with the Bible — or at least a good portion of it. You may or may not wish to memorize verses, but you will want to discover the main stories, the important people and their places. With time and consistency those passages significant for you will become part of your inner vocabulary. They will come to your mind when you need them. You may not remember exactly where a certain sentence is found but that need not disturb you. One young priest said, "I don't have the gift of numbers" to remember chapter and verse, so he bought a concord- ance. With it, he could always find what he needed.

The kind of familiarity we need for inner growth may not always be specific. It is more a developing current that increasingly underlies our daily awareness. Scripture becomes an atmosphere in which we breathe and eat and work and pray. Words, verses, stories, and teachings arise in our memory as we live, as we pray more deeply, as we grow into communion with God.

When we feel lovingly familiar with a section of Scripture, we can even play with it appreciatively, as we play with a child. For example, when I lived in the Arizona desert and summer came on dry and hot, we were always scanning the sky for signs of rain. Eventually, sure enough, there would be a "cloud the size of a man's hand."

What's that? It's what Elijah looked for (which is why I always thought we should pray to him for rain). When? Why? Who's Elijah anyway? Really curious? Go look it up (1 Kings 17:1— 2 Kings 2:13).

Our point is not Elijah himself. It is to show that familiarity with the Bible enriches our life, becomes part of us, supports us, guides us, challenges us — and even plays with us.

Deepening Our Awareness

As we read the Bible and pray with its verses, if we look especially for inner meanings, we come to a deeper level of awareness, both of Scripture and of ourselves. This happens as we ask, "What does this mean for my inner life, for my relationship with God?" That is quite different from asking, "Did this really happen the way it's written?" (That question is all right, but it has a more external focus.)

With attention turned to inner life, we see new light on Scrip- tures, from Ecclesiastes to the gospels. Take Psalm 109:6-9ff, for example:

Raise up a wicked man against him,
   and let the accuser stand at his right hand.
When he is judged, let him go forth condemned,
   and may his plea be in vain.
May his days be few;
   may another take his office.
May his children be fatherless,
   and his wife a widow....

Taken at the surface level, this is bitter vengeance. But suppose the enemy here is an inner enemy, some quality in our hearts that keeps us from God. Then how does it read?

Some of the so-called "hard sayings" of Jesus also have a powerful impact when interior meanings are sought rather than external or behavioral ones.

Another way to approach inner meanings is to ask, "If everyone in this passage is some part of myself, what does the Lord offer here?" Jesus' parables and other teachings are doubly powerful when approached in this way.

Challenged to Grow

As we live with the Bible, we allow its words to challenge us. We need not trap ourselves in guilt. Rather, we can accept biblical challenges as directions for a spiritual practice or suggestions for reaching a new depth in God. If we do not understand something, it may be because the passage is difficult, but it may also be because we have not yet lived our way into the meaning of that text. Much of the inner significance of Scripture will open itself only to those who are developing spiritually.

The longer and more deeply one lives in the atmosphere of Scripture, the more it illumines our experiences and the more our living illumines its meaning. A vigorous dialogue arises between the deepening of our inner life and the deeper recognition of biblical meanings that seem new to us because we were not ready to see them earlier. In this sense, the Word of God is a gentle teacher. We will perceive truly only what we are ready to apply in our life.

Of course, if we then do not practice what we have been given, further understanding will be limited. Often enough I have wanted more understanding, only to realize that I had not yet internalized the insights already granted to me. This clogged communication with the Word, so I had to step back and put life-in-God first yet again. As I was able to receive, new awareness was given once more.

It is like a winding staircase leading to a level we vaguely know. But to see it fully and feel it in our whole self, we have to walk the stairs. We may choose to rest at a certain step, but when we do, our vision of the top rests also at its present incomplete state. When we continually apply our insights from Scripture, it does indeed become for us a living Word.

Only as Scripture became life for the great mystical saints did it also become companion, strength, motivation, and real guidance.

So there are two keys to drawing from Scripture what we need for our journey. One is consistent and deepening familiarity. The other is ever-ready willingness to practice what we do understand. The keys are simple enough, aren't they? Yet, because it is God's Word and not just any word, the Bible will walk ahead of us all the way to our home in God's heart.

For Your Reflection

1. Go treasure-troving at random in Proverbs, Wisdom, and Sirach.
2. Read Bible stories aloud to the family or spouse.
3. Memorize favorite passages.
4. Choose one gospel and read it through, twice a week for a month (eight times).

5. Choose a book of the Bible you do not remember reading or hearing and read it.
6. Following are passages that will aid in appreciating Scripture.

   2 Timothy 3:14-17
   Romans 15:4-5
   Mark 4:1-9, 14-20
   Psalm 119:18, 30-32, 41-48, 105, 165
   Psalm 19:8-11

CHAPTER TWELVE

The Mass:
Reflection of
Our Final Goal

For us Catholic Christians, the Mass is already a familiar part of our living pattern. It is so familiar that our participation is sometimes quite mechanical. We tend to "come to" our congregational responses, then fade away again into dreams and worries and watching the children two rows ahead.

Yet for some, the Mass is the focus of all that is meaningful. Their attention is concentrated, and they look for empowering interior ways to participate. They find their treasure in the Mass.

Recently, it dawned on me that the Mass is a microcosm of our spiritual life. It can re-center us each time we participate, provided we do so consciously. By honing our concentration, we can discover new treasures in the Mass. Let us examine its pattern and see how it reflects recurring patterns in our spiritual journey. (You may wish to follow along in a missal as you read this.)

Penitence and Praise

Our first act in the Mass is penitence. We acknowledge our failings and seek the Lord's mercy. For many people this same inner impulse initiates spiritual growth. We recognize our feelings of distance and separation from God. We know it has to do with habits, choices, and attitudes that do not match the standards of Jesus. So we bring them to the Lord and ask forgiveness. The Lord always receives us. Thus begins our spiritual journey.

Once begun, it begins again and again. Every time we rediscover the discrepancies between our living and our goal, we turn to the Lord for mercy and healing. At the penitential rite of the Mass, we ask pardon formally and regularly. It is a wonderful time to realign ourselves with God's intention, to strengthen us, and to remind us if we have been forgetful.

Then comes the Gloria, a hymn of highest praise to the Lord. Truly in our spiritual growth, each time we turn toward God again, we feel only gratitude. We discover anew how great is the God who receives us so mercifully. As our communion with him deepens, we become ever more grateful, even awed, as we seek him daily. Praise wells up within us increasingly as we grow. It becomes an undercurrent of attitude, supporting our everyday activities. In our daily practice, we may simply sigh our thanks. At Mass we sing it with full hearts.

Supported by His Word

Next the Mass turns to scriptural readings and the homily. Scripture reading is already supporting our spiritual growth. Our familiarity with Scripture will strengthen our experience at Mass. Attention to these readings will also strengthen our regular reading practice.

The readings are intended for our support, instruction, inspiration, and insight. We need instruction because we can never know enough to find the way alone. We need inspiration because we tend to be lazy and forgetful of our goal. We need insight because we are so often blind to our real interior situation.

We find these helps in other people, in books about God and the spiritual life, in nature, in quiet examination of our own living, in prayer and contemplation, in the creative expression of the arts. We learn to be alert to God's guidance and encouragement everywhere. One friend even finds help in the shapes of clouds. Our increasing awareness of God helps us to see him in all things. In the Mass we may experience these helps at any moment, but they are particularly intended in the readings.

We then listen to a homily, the reflections of our priest or deacon on the Scriptures. Ideally, the homily will be well-prepared, well-crafted, and prayed over. But it may not be. There is a danger here. We can lean far too heavily on the homily to provide the highest moment of the Mass for us. If we do that, we do an injustice to ourselves and our homilist, and we miss the true high point of the Mass.

The power of the Mass is not dependent on the personality or talents or style of the homilist or the celebrant. If the homily is good, that is a wonderful bonus. If it is not, then our spiritual life can grow by loving our homilist as he does his duty. Thus, we make another step toward God and lessen the burden of our earthly shepherd as well.

Our Offerings

When we have lovingly heard and received the spoken Word, we respond by praying for others and by offering ourselves to God.

In the spiritual life, we are keenly aware of how little we can do for others without prayer, but how powerful praying for others is. Surely, everyone who has prayed through the years for the "conversion of Russia" rejoices in the power of prayer.

As we assimilate the inspiration of the Scriptures in our individual spirituality, we turn naturally to prayer for individuals and issues close to our hearts. One of the powerful breakthroughs in my own spiritual journey came after six weeks of praying intensely for God's mercy for the whole world. Although it seemed too big a prayer project for me, it opened a huge door in my own spirit. Prayer for others is vital to our own spiritual growth.

So is offering ourselves. When we give money at the offertory, we are not just paying our priest or painting the building. In our society, money touches us almost more than anything. We can talk about our bedroom and bathroom and not blink, but who else knows how much money we make? Money is deeply tied to our ego, our self-image, our dreams, and our fears. When we give this symbol of our very selves, we offer our most intimate self to the heart of God.

Self-offering is ultimately the only way we can be united with God. The giving over of our entire self to God will not happen (for most of us) for a long time. It may be hard even to imagine. So we practice along the way. We give our work to God. We give our talents. We give our fears. We give our relationships. Little by little, we offer more and more of ourselves. In that spirit we offer our money — and ourselves in that money — to God in the Mass.

Receiving Christ

Then comes the magnificent eucharistic prayer. In it we express our deep honoring of God, recalling again all he has done in our lives, from creation until this very day. Such worship is integral to every relationship with God. The four familiar eucharistic prayers of the Mass are strong and beautiful. They deserve study. They can lift our minds away from distractions and put everything into perspective once again. This ever-repeated return to the splendor of God must penetrate all our spiritual growth. The eucharistic prayer offers us a formal opportunity.

Then we remember and reenact the great sacrifice that made everything else possible. The fullness of everything Christ is comes again to particularize itself on our altar and enter our inmost being.

A newly discovered analogy for Christ in the Eucharist had fresh impact on me. It may not be found in a theology book, but I think it is a true analogy. It is a hologram: a picture taken in such a way that it shows three dimensions of the photographed object when illumined by a laser beam. You can walk around such a picture and see all sides. Even more fascinating, when that picture is physically broken into small pieces, every piece contains the whole picture, completely visible again with the laser. The consecrated host and wine are like hologram of Jesus — totally there, no matter how small the piece.

We receive Communion and assimilate it into our whole being. It is a reality at whatever level we receive it. It is a foretaste of our final goal — complete reception of God, fully pervading our being. This transformative union with the Trinity is the hope of our lives, the birthright of every Christian.

Love Is the Reason

The key element of this powerful sacrifice is love. It originated in divine love and continues to bring God's love, his very nature, deep into our being. This is the only sensible reason to go to Mass. We participate in the Mass to offer love to God and to receive God's love into our hearts. The impulse to love God is his love.

So also in the spiritual journey. There is only one reason to undertake this journey, only one reason to continue it: the love of God. Love — divine, powerful, available — is the reason for the universe. It is the core of everything we experience, of everything we hope for, and potentially of everything we do. When the Eucharist and our individual spiritual development meet and mingle, there is only love. Love becomes, if only for a moment, everything for us.

Experiencing the Mass in this way, every participation is a chance for another turn in the upward spiral of our spiritual journey. The Mass will carry us within it just as much as we carry the Mass in our awareness all the way to God's own heart. We grow in our relationship with God all week. Then we take it to him formally, with the whole Church. In turn we carry the power of that Mass into our growth for the next week, a pattern and promise of what is to come.

Thus experienced, the Mass will carry us when we cannot walk, go ahead to lead us when we can. In whatever our circumstances, the Mass is there to express our spirituality and to deepen our life in God. It is a miniature of our whole journey into the divine heart.

For Your Reflection

1. Get a missal and study the Mass.
2. Watch the flux of your attention during Mass.
3. Pray for the celebrant all through a Mass.
4. Try to be fully aware of Christ at the moment of receiving Communion.
5. Here are Scripture passages to help better understand and love the Mass.

   Psalms 8:1-10; 34:1-4
   Matthew 3:1-2
   Romans 12:1
   Luke 22:19
   Revelation 2:4-5
   Ephesians 6:18
   Hebrews 13:15-16
   1 John 4:7-21

CONCLUSION

These reflections are only a hint at the inner riches of a life dedicated primarily to God's Holy Spirit of transformation. Every pilgrim on this astounding journey will experience it in a particular fashion and will emphasize one or another practice. Only a few of the possibilities are mentioned in this book.

Each person on the journey will travel inward in a style appropriate to personal characteristics and needs. One may walk with dignity, calm and steady, maybe accompanied by Gregorian chant. Another may scamper lightly from one wonder to another, exclaiming, "Oh, *look* at this one!" Yet another may travel slowly with great labor, shouldering the burdens of others along the way. One may seem to be carried along by friends and teachers, helped in every way. For some the journey is taken in company, while many are isolated pilgrims.

Because each person's way is different, we are wise not to compare ourselves to others we meet. Comparison almost always asks: Who is better, who perhaps is further on the journey? When we compare, we either feel diminished because we are slow or puffed up because we seem better. Neither is helpful. We are wise to learn and appreciate our own God-given style. Each pilgrim is made to travel the way he or she can. That is always more than good enough; the important thing is that we go.

No matter what the style of travel might be, the goal is the same and there are common elements to each person's journey.

The goal for all is fullness of life in the heart of God. We pray to be established in union with the Holy Trinity. That is an awesome prayer, and yet this is the birthright of every Christian. Today, we do see that it is offered by Jesus Christ to each person who is thirsty for deeper communion with God.

We do not know exactly what life would be like if lived in union with God. We have the witness of saints through the centuries, and glimpses are given to every pilgrim on the way. The goal is absolute love, without preference for this person or that person and regardless of "worthiness." Love is love, given freely and without price to all. Many have not believed that this depth and constancy of love is possible in this life. Yet human beings, children of God as we may become, are called to it and many have experienced life in this wondrous intensity. As love is the inner dynamic of the Trinity, so love is the force pervading one's very existence. We are to learn to see it, receive it, and give it without reserve. That is the aim we follow, the "city" we hope to enter.

Along the way, love opens our hearts a little here and a little there. Swift insights come that hint at the glory of loving all equally in all moments and all experiences. Sometimes love on the way is experienced as a flash of joy, a period of comfort. Other times it stands before us, a challenge and a test. Love is seldom what we expect; it is nearly always more, deeper, brighter, stronger.

The saints tell us that the way to God is not easy. Each of us is born with a sense of separation from others, from life, from God. We feel an intense individuality, as if our being and our potential stopped at our skin and we were forever encapsulated in this little body. We cling to this sense of "I-ness," even though we are told repeatedly that it is in fact the greatest barrier to the grace of God taking over our heart.

The difficulties of the inner journey have a common root. In these reflections I have called it "ego," that quality in each of us that is separate, frightened, possessive, unloving, and all the rest. This ego in our being is powerful, and we continually give it more power, until we embark on the spiritual journey. Then, little by little, we begin to remove our small, selfish ego from the center of power and allow God gradually to take over that central place.

It is never easy to see this root of our difficulty, but honesty and sincere practice can show it to us. Then we know clearly that the battle must be engaged if we are to come close to God. In this intense inner effort, where joy and pain often live simultaneously, we are never abandoned. God is always present in the thick of it. The trick is to remember he is there and to cast ourselves on his mercy, trusting entirely in his grace to give us what we need to prevail over our own selfishness. He will always sustain our journey, even when we forget to ask him for help.

Our common prayer from beginning to end is that the Holy Spirit be constantly aware of us, even when we forget what we are about, and that we never be allowed to stop our progress on the journey. We pray that we be true to the way, that we be brought back from side trips and protected from all real injuries. We need not ask never to make mistakes — they are our lessons — and they are always with us. We will stumble often enough and fall headlong sometimes, but truly those lessons become our strength and power for the next hill, the next challenge. Nothing is without its purpose in this pilgrimage to God. No event is without its gift. We only want to keep going. We pray for the grace to continue. We pray for the inner power of God to sustain us in the journey and to hold our inner eye firmly on the magnificence of our goal.

In the beginning of our inward journey into God, we have the witness of others, especially Jesus, and our own longing to draw us forward. As we take a step at a time, more and more of God is given us in his loving grace. Gradually, we experience new strength, new vision. To this journey there will be no end. As Saint Gregory of Nyssa insisted, "God is infinite and therefore this spiritual unfolding into his heart is also infinite."

From our first "yes" to the splendor beyond every imagining, we can rely on one thing: "I will not leave you orphans; I will come to you....On that day you will realize that I am in my Father and you are in me and I in you" (John 14:18, 20).

May the journey be glorious for each of you!